A long time ago,
As a little girl,
I dreamed of traveling
All over the world ...

... And often I'd ask about the past
Driving everyone crazy fast!
Amused by this my parents thought,
Why not call me "History" for short?

Dedicated to
GEORGE IRELAND
My Uncle
& Godfather

BARBARA ANN MOJICA'S

Little Miss HISTORY ®

Travels to

MOUNT VERNON

Illustrations by VICTOR RAMON MOJICA

Who do you think of when you hear the name George Washington –

... first president of The United States, or military hero of the American Revolution?

Actually, George Washington preferred life on the farm at his plantation in Mount Vernon, Virginia. Slaves used a scythe like this one to cut the Mansion lawn called the bowling green.

Samuel Vaughan, an English architect, visited Mount Vernon in 1787. He drew a design for George Washington known as ...

... the "Vaughan Plan." That plan provides a key to understanding what the grounds at Mount Vernon looked like when Washington lived there.

Mount Vernon contained 8,000 acres divided into five farms. One of them held the Mansion House.

In the foyer of
the Mansion House there
is a large key enclosed
in a glass case.

It's a gift from
Washington's friend the
Marquis de Lafayette.

The French people used this key
to storm the Bastille prison in 1789
to win their independence.

Washington's visitors dined in the "New Room," one of his favorite rooms. His diary shows that almost 700 visitors stayed overnight at the Mansion in just one year.

Upstairs are several bedchambers.
One famous room is the "Chintz Room."

It was called the "Chintz Room"
because of its floral print decor.

In Washington's bedroom is a customized bed ...

... made for him.

He stood six foot two.

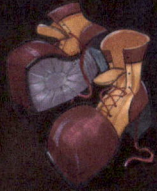

Washington kept his clothing in his private study, where he read, wrote letters and conducted business.

Bathrooms did not exist inside the house.

"Necessary Houses" were located outside.

Washington loved trees and gardens.
The upper garden included a greenhouse with
a radiant heating system under the floor.

It burned down in
1835. Harry S. Truman,
33rd President of the
United States, donated
bricks from the White
House renovation to
rebuild the greenhouse
in 1951.

A lower garden raised fruit and vegetables to be used in the kitchen.

George Washington's wife, Martha, needed a separate building for her large kitchen. She managed it with a hired supervisor and several slaves.

Two walking lanes to the north and south of the Mansion House kept the outside buildings out of sight. About 85 slaves lived and worked along here.

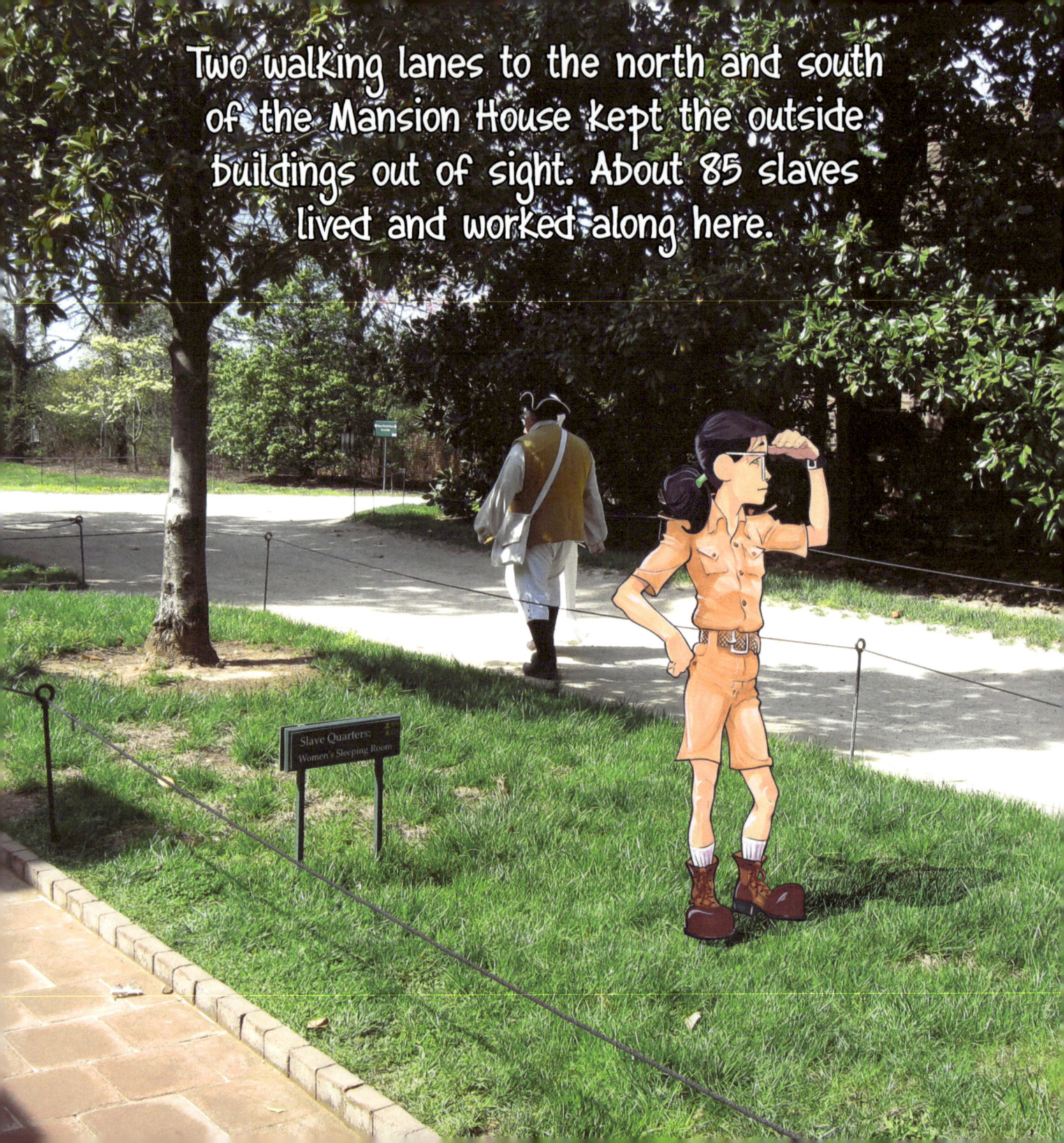

Slave Quarters:
Women's Sleeping Room

In a coach house and stable, slaves
like Peter Hardiman fed and groomed animals,
cleaned harnesses, saddles,
and collected manure for fertilizer.

Joe drove travel vehicles like this coach ...

... and riding chair, while Jack fixed the wagons.

A smokehouse nearby
held fowl, fish,
salted and pickled meats
for preservation.

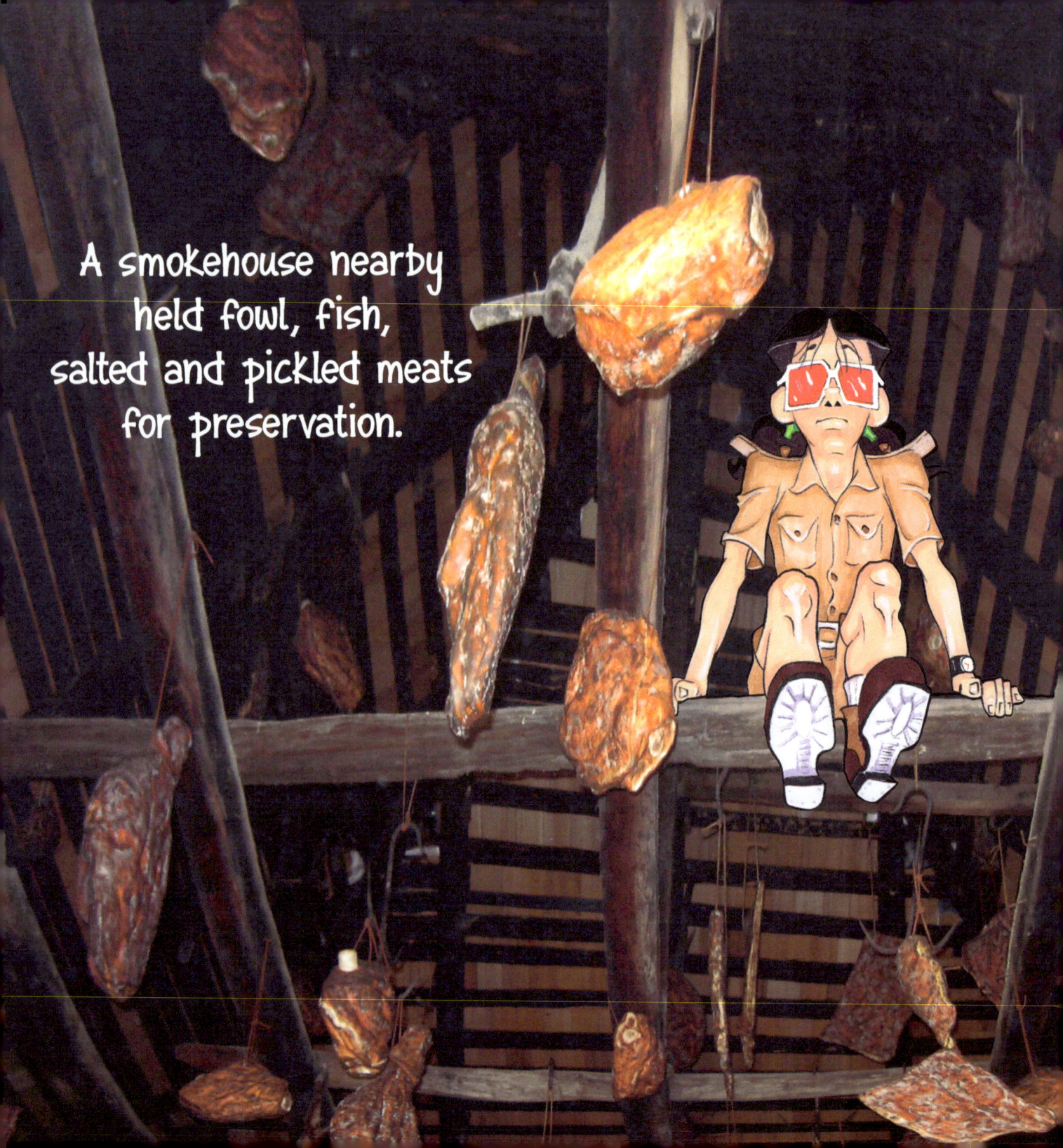

There were no refrigerators
or running water inside homes.

The Mansion House cellar probably had a kitchen for slaves. Wine, whiskey, brandy, and food items were stored here too.

A shoemaker made shoes in his shop. Each slave received only one pair of shoes for the year.

Men and women
lived in separate
slave quarters.

Each dwelling included bed
pallets with a few necessities.

Slaves labored from sunrise to sunset, with only a few holidays and Sundays off.

Washington accepted slavery,
but he did not allow harsh
treatment of his slaves.
Yet none were freed
until his death.

George Washington believed it was the government's responsiblity to end slavery in America.

Do you think he was right?

After inspecting his farm on a cold, wet, wintry day he failed to change his clothes. Washington died suddenly on December 14, 1799, after developing a throat infection.

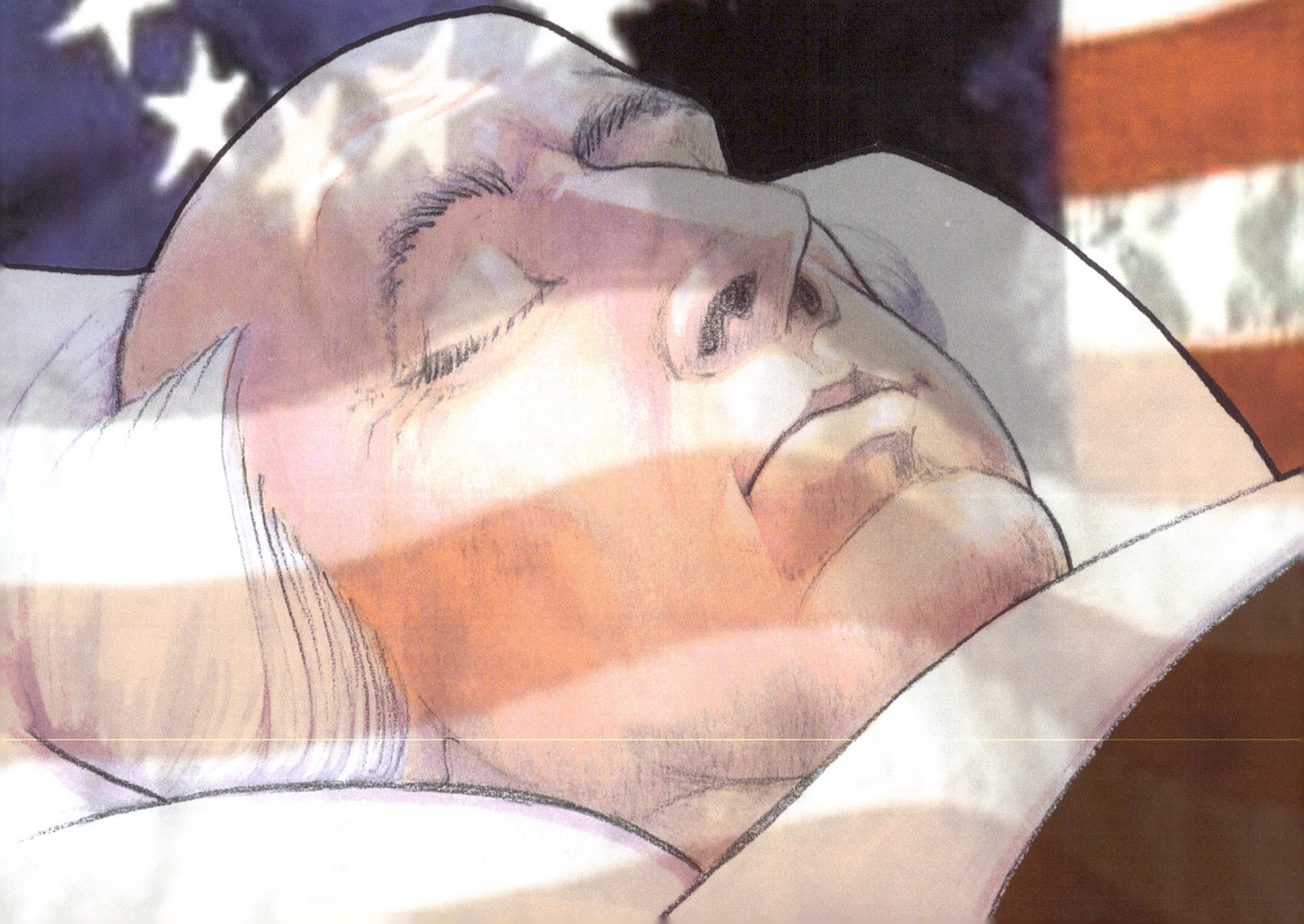

Washington dictated his burial plans in his will. He asked that a new brick vault be built next to his fruit garden and nursery for himself and family ...

... but Congress desired a memorial and tomb in Washington D.C. Ultimately the family refused. In 1831 the bodies were moved to the new vault at Mount Vernon.

In his will, Washington also left instructions to free the slaves that were his personal property.

Slaves who worked at Mount Vernon were buried in unmarked graves on a hillside nearby.

In 1929 The Mount Vernon Ladies Association set up the first U.S. memorial for slaves.

IN MEMORY OF
THE AFRO AMERICANS
WHO SERVED AS SLAVES
AT MOUNT VERNON
THIS MONUMENT MARKING THEIR
BURIAL GROUND
DEDICATED
SEPTEMBER 21, 1983
MOUNT VERNON
LADIES' ASSOCIATION

It was replaced with a larger one designed by students from Howard University in 1983.

Before leaving Mount Vernon
be sure to visit the
DONALD W. REYNOLDS
Museum and Education Center.

There you will learn more
about Mount Vernon
and George Washington's
personal life.

NEXT STOP...

LA BREA
TAR
PITS
& MUSEUM

Don't Miss
Little Miss HISTORY'S
Other Adventures ...

... Wherever
Books Are Sold!